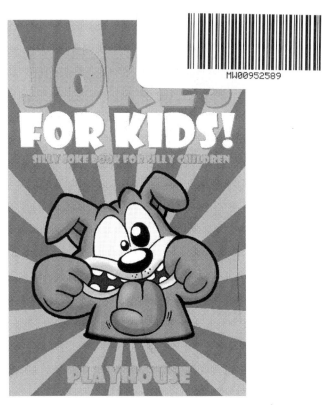

Thank YOU!

Thank you for purchasing the book. Playhouse takes pride in providing the best collection of books for children. We welcome all feedback and suggestions so please feel free to leave a review of the book on amazon.

Question:

Why do giraffes have such long necks?

Answer:

Because their feet are stinky!

Question:

What animal has to wear a wig?

Answer:

The bald eagle!

Question:

What is a snake's favorite school subject?

Answer:

Hissssss-story!

Question:

What do you call a bull in a deep sleep?

Answer:

A bull-dozer!

Question:

What is a frog's favorite year?

Answer:

Leap Years!

Question:

Why did the cow cross the road?

Answer:

To reach the udder side!

Question:

What do you call a bear with no teeth?

Answer:

A gummy bear!

Question:

What do large whales eat?

Answer:

Fish and ships!

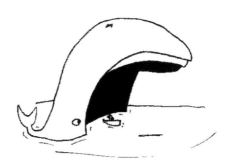

Question:

Why did the dinosaur cross the road?

Answer:

Because chickens were not around yet!

Question:

What do alligator's drink?

Answer:

Gator-Ade!

Question:

How do you count a lot of cows?

Answer:

With a cow-culator!

Question:

What is the strongest animal in the world?

Answer:

A snail! They carry their house!

Question:

What type of cat should you never play a game with?

Answer:

A cheetah!

Question:

What did the buffalo say to his son before he went to school?

Answer:

Bison!

Question:

How do mice feel after taking a bath?

Answer:

Squeaky clean!

Question:

What is a puppy's favorite pizza?

Answer:

Pupperoni!

Question:

How do bees get to school?

Answer:

They take the school buzz!

Question:

Why does the ocean shine and twinkle at night?

Answer:

Because it's full of starfish!

Question:

What is a cheetah's favorite type of food?

Answer:

Fast food!

Question:

What is a cat's favorite breakfast?

Answer:

Mice krispies!

Question:

What is the biggest ant in the world?

Answer:

An eleph-ant!

Question:

How does a dog stop a video?

Answer:

By pressing paws!

Question:

What type of dog always has a fever?

Answer:

A hot dog!

Question:

What do you call a snake not wearing any clothes?

Answer:

Snaked!

Question:

Why did the sheep get a ticket from the policeman?

Answer:

The sheep was a baaaaaaaaaad driver!

Question:

What sounds does a cat make if you accidentally step on its tail?

Answer:

Me-ow!

Question:

What did one cow say to the other cow blocking his way?

Answer:

Mooooooooove over!

Question:

Why do some cows have to wear bells
around their neck?

Answer:

Because their horns don't work!

Question:

Why are mice so afraid of water?

Answer:

Because of catfish!

Question:

Why are leopards not very good at hide and seek?

Answer:

Because they're always spotted!

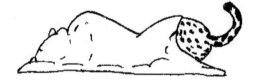

Question:

What is a shark's favorite food?

Answer:

A peanut butter and jellyfish sandwich!

Question:

What soda do frogs drink?

Answer:

Croak-a-cola!

Question:

What do dogs say to the fleas?

Answer:

Stop bugging me!

Question:

What did the porcupine say to the cactus?

Answer:

Are you my mommy?

Question:

What do you call a horse that lives next door to you?

Answer:

Your neigh-bor!

Question:

How do bees greet one another?

Answer:

They say wasabi!

Question:

What does a dog do if he loses his tail?

Answer:

He will go shopping at the re-tail store!

Question:

What do you call a bunch of rabbits hopping backwards?

Answer:

A receding hare-line!

Question:

What do you get if cross a fish and an elephant?

Answer:

Swimming trunks!

Question:

Why do pandas prefer older movies?

Answer:

Because older movies are black and white!

Question:

What do you call a scrap on a t-rex?

Answer:

A dino-sore!

Question:

What happens if you cross a centipede with a parrot?

Answer:

You get a walkie talkie!

Question:

How can a kangaroo jump higher than the tallest building?

Answer:

Because buildings cannot jump!

Question:

What is the name for a messy hippo?

Answer:

A hippopota-mess!

Question:

Why can you never believe the king of the jungle?

Answer:

Because he's always lion!

Question:

How can you make an octopus laugh?

Answer:

With ten-tickles!

Question:

Why are cats afraid of trees?

Answer:

Because of the bark!

Question:

How do fish save money?

Answer:

In a river bank!

Question:

Why did young boy eat his homework?

Answer:

His teacher told him it is a piece of cake!

Question:

What can you give to a sick lemon?

Answer:

Lemon aid!

Question:

What do you get when you cross a shellfish and an apple?

Answer:

A crab apple!

Question:

Why did the cookie go to the hospital?

Answer:

Because it was feeling crummy!

Question:

What do you call two banana peels on the floor?

Answer:

A pair of slippers!

Question:

What did the plate say to the spoon?

Answer:

Dinner is on me!

Question:

What do you call a sleeping pizza?

Answer:

A piZZZZZZZa!

Question:

What do you call cheese that does not belong to you?

Answer:

Nacho cheese!

Question:

Why kind of food can increase your eyesight?

Answer:

Seafood!

Question:

What did the mayonnaise say to the refrigerator?

Answer:

Shut the door! I'm dressing!

Question:

Why do donuts go to the dentist?

Answer:

To get chocolate fillings!

Question:

What did the teddy bear say when offered more food?

Answer:

No thanks, I'm stuffed!

Question:

Why do seagulls fly over the sea?

Answer:

**Because they would be called bagels
if they flew over the bay!**

Question:

Why are nosey peppers so annoying?

Answer:

Because they get jalapeno business!

Question:

What do you call a caring french fry?

Answer:

A sweet potato!

Question:

When a potato has a baby, what do you call the babies?

Answer:

Tater tots!

Question:

What's in an astronaut's favourite type of sandwich?

Answer:

A Launch meat sandwich!

Question:

What kind of lettuce did people eat on the Titanic?

Answer:

Iceberg!

Question:

Why do hamburgers go to the gym?

Answer:

To beef up!

Question:

What kind of key is edible?

Answer:

A cookie!

Question:

What do firefighters eat with their soup?

Answer:

Firecrackers!

Question:

Why would a potato be a good detective?

Answer:

Because potatoes keep their eyes peeled!

Question:

What do trees drink?

Answer:

Root beer!

Question:

What did one sandwich say to another sandwich telling a fib?

Answer:

You're full of bologna!

Question:

Why do some people stare at bottles of orange juice?

Answer:

Because the bottles say concentrate!

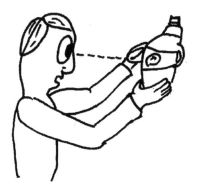

Question:

How do you fix a broken pumpkin?

Answer:

With a pumpkin patch!

Question:

What should a hotdog do if it misses
too much school?

Answer:

Stay after school to ketchup!

Question:

How do you fix a cracked tomato?

Answer:

By using tomato paste!

Question:

What is another name for a train full of bubble gum?

Answer:

A chew-chew train!

Question:

What happens if you cross a Christmas tree and an apple?

Answer:

You get a Pineapple!

Question:

Why did the banana visit the hospital?

Answer:

**Because the banana wasn't peeling
very well!**

Question:

What kind of food can you find at the beach?

Answer:

A SANDwich!

Question:

What is Dracula's favorite fruit?

Answer:

Blood Oranges!

Question:

What did the baby corn say to his mommy?

Answer:

Where's popcorn?

Question:

What is orange and sounds like parrot?

Answer:

A carrot!

Question:

What do you get when too many blueberries try to go through a door at the same time?

Answer:

A Blueberry Jam!

Question:

Why do ghosts always feel hungry?

Answer:

Because food goes right through them!

Question:

How do lollipops say goodbye to one another?

Answer:

Bye-bye, sucker!

Question:

What's a pretzel's favorite dance move?

Answer:

The twist!

Question:

What do you call cheese that is cold?

Answer:

Chili cheese!

Question:

Why didn't the fish share his food?

Answer:

Because he was shellfish!

Question:

Why shouldn't eggs tell jokes?

Answer:

Because they'd crack each other up!

Question:

What is the name for a fake noodle?

Answer:

An Impasta!

Question:

What do mice like to eat for their birthdays??

Answer:

Cheesecake!!

Question:

Why didn't the pizza tell good jokes?

Answer:

It was too cheesy!

Question:

Why do golfers always have two pairs
of pants?

Answer:

In case they got a hole in one!

Question:

How does a baseball glove say goodbye to a baseball?

Answer:

Catch you later!

Question:

Why do you want a bowling alley to be quiet?

Answer:

So you are able to hear a pin drop!

Question:

What happens if a dinosaur kicks a ball
into a goal?

Answer:

A dino-score!

Question:

How are baseball teams and pancakes similar?

Answer:

They both need a good batter!

Question:

Why do football players get hot after a game?

Answer:

All of the fans go away!

Question:

Why is tennis such a loud sport?

Answer:

Because the players raise a racquet!

Question:

What is a swimmer's favorite subject in math?

Answer:

Dive-ision!

Question:

What type of shirts do golfers wear?

Answer:

Tee shirts!

Question:

What drink do athletic boxers drink?

Answer:

Punch!

Question:

A skater slipped, what did she say to the ice?

Answer:

I'm going to let it slide this time!

Question:

When is cross country skiing easy?

Answer:

If you live in a small country!

Question:

What do baseball players eat on?

Answer:

Home plates!

Question:

Where do basketball players go when they needs a new uniform?

Answer:

New Jersey!

Question:

What is a hairstylist's favorite sport?

Answer:

Curling!

Question:

Why are babies good at basketball?

Answer:

Because they are good at dribbling!

Question:

What do bowlers and baseball players argue over?

Answer:

What a strike is!

Question:

Why was the football player bowling?

Answer:

Because he was in the Super Bowl!

Question:

What can you serve but shouldn't eat?

Answer:

A tennis ball!

Question:

Why is it hard to play sports with a pig?

Answer:

Because it will always hog the ball!

Question:

What's an insect's favorite sport?

Answer:

Cricket!

Question:

Why did the vampires have to cancel the baseball game?

Answer:

Because they were not able to find their bats!

Question:

Why is it a bad idea to tell jokes while you skate?

Answer:

Because you might make the ice crack up!

Question:

What animal is best at hitting a baseball?

Answer:

A bat!

Question:

What do golfers drink?

Answer:

Tee!

Question:

Why did the hockey player go to college?

Answer:

It was his goal!

Question:

Why did the boy bring string to the baseball game?

Answer:

He thought he could tie up the game!

Question:

What did the janitor say when he jumped out to scare someone?

Answer:

Supplies!

Question:

Why do girl scouts sell cookies?

Answer:

To make a sweet first impression!

Question:

What did the judge say when the smelly skunk walked into the court room?

Answer:

Odor in the court!

Question:

How can you find a Princess?

Answer:

Just follow the foot Prince!

Question:

Why did the one handed man cross the road?

Answer:

To get to the second hand shop!

Question:

Why was the guy looking for food everywhere on his friend?

Answer:

Because his friend said lunch is on me!

Question:

What does judge ask a dentist in court?

Answer:

Do you swear to pull the tooth, the whole tooth and nothing but the tooth!

Question:

Where is an astronaut's favorite place on a computer?

Answer:

At the space bar!

Question:

Why did the boy leave sugar all over his pillow before sleeping?

Answer:

He wanted to have sweet dreams!

Question:

What dance move should all astronauts know?

Answer:

The moonwalk!

Question:

Why are pirates called pirates?

Answer:

Because they arrrrr!

Question:

Why couldn't the pirate play with his cards?

Answer:

Because he was sitting on the deck!

Question:

Why did the girl throw her clock out of the window?

Answer:

Because she wanted to see time fly!

Question:

How do hairstylists make their job quicker?

Answer:

They take short cuts!

Question:

Why did the scientist remove her doorbell?

Answer:

She wanted to win the no-bell prize!

Question:

How do prisoners call each other?

Answer:

Cell phones!

Question:

What time do most people visit the dentist?

Answer:

At tooth-hurty!

Question:

What type of shoes should all spies wear?

Answer:

Sneak-ers!

Question:

Why did the boy put all his money in the freezer?

Answer:

He wanted cold hard cash!

Question:

What do all lawyers wear in court?

Answer:

Lawsuits!

Question:

What does the dentist of the year get?

Answer:

A little plaque!

Question:

What do you call two witches that share an apartment?

Answer:

Broom-mates!

Question:

What is the first thing elves learn in school?

Answer:

The elf-abet!

Question:

What's the worst part about having a party in space?

Answer:

You must planet!

Question:

Why did the skeleton not attend the dance?

Answer:

He had no body to dance with!

Question:

Why is 6 afraid of 7?

Answer:

Because 7 8 9!

Question:

What musical instrument do skeletons play?

Answer:

The trom-bone!

Question:

A boomerang that does not come back
to you is called what?

Answer:

A stick!

Question:

What did the scarf say to the hat?

Answer:

You go ahead, I'll hang around!

Question:

What do you call an old snowman?

Answer:

Water!

Question:

What has four wheels and flies?

Answer:

Garbage trucks!

Question:

Which flower always talks the most?

Answer:

Tulips, because they have two lips!

Question:

Why do rocks from the moon taste better than rocks from earth?

Answer:

Because they're meteor!

Question:

Why did the drum take a nap?

Answer:

It was beat!

Question:

How do billboards communicate with each other?

Answer:

Sign language!

Question:

Why couldn't the bike stand up on its own?

Answer:

Because it was too tired!

Question:

What did the penny say to the other penny?

Answer:

We make perfect cents!

Question:

How does the ocean say hello?

Answer:

It waves!

Question:

Have you heard the joke about the butter?

Answer:

I shouldn't tell you, it might spread!

Question:

Why was the math book so sad?

Answer:

It had too many problems!

Question:

What did one eye say to the other?

Answer:

Just between me and you, something smells!

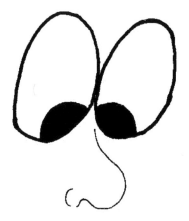

Question:

What two things can you not have at breakfast?

Answer:

Lunch and dinner!

Question:

What does an ill bucket say to another bucket?

Answer:

I am feeling pale today!

Question:

What do walls often say to each other?

Answer:

I'll meet you at the corner!

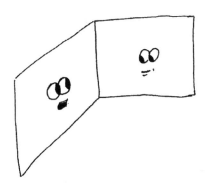

Question:

Where do pencils go to when on vacation?

Answer:

Pencil-vania!

Question:

What season would you use a trampoline most?

Answer:

Spring time!

Question:

Why was the picture put behind bars in jail?

Answer:

It was framed!

Question:

What do trees say to the wind?

Answer:

Leaf us alone!

Question:

How can you make a tissue dance?

Answer:

By giving it a little boogie!

Question:

What do you call a funny mountain?

Answer:

Hill-arious!

Question:

What happens if you cross a snowman
and a vampire?

Answer:

You get a frostbite!

Question:

What washes up on very small
beaches?

Answer:

Micro-waves!

Question:

What did the triangle say to the circle?

Answer:

You're pointless!

Question:

What school teaches you how to say hello to people?

Answer:

Hi school!

Question:

Why did the computer go to the doctor?

Answer:

It had a virus!

Question:

What's a mummies favorite music?

Answer:

Wrap music!

Made in the USA
Columbia, SC
23 January 2019